FastTrack™

The Complete Course

FastTrack™

The Complete Course

Gaining A Big-Picture View of the

National Board Certification Process for Teachers

by Joetta M. Schneider, NBCT

Printed in the United States of America

ISBN-13: 978-0-692-12674-5

ISBN-10: 0692126740

Other Resources from My National Board:

- The FastTrackTM Course (Individual Chapters 1-4) for teachers who want a quick understanding of each component

- "Five"— National Board Prep Course™

- Renewal—a short overview for NBCTs who want to renew their certification

- My National Board™ Workshops— on site workshops including FastTrackTM, Five™, Train-the-Trainer, and National Board Overview; we can personalize a workshop to your needs

- NB Academic Coaching via phone, Skype, or in-person

If you need anything associated with these resources, or have questions we may be able to answer, feel free to contact us at: MyNationalBoard.com

Email us at info@mynationalboard.com

Find us on FaceBook @My National Board for Teachers

Contents

Acknowledgments

This book is dedicated to Jenny Santilli and Elissa Whelchel, who attended every meeting and planning session for four school years to make the Harrison County NBCT Candidate Support Cohort happen.

It's further dedicated to the Inklings, of which Jenny and Elissa are a part, as well as Connie Bowers, Missy Hinerman, and Stephanie Runion. To fellow NBCT Nerds Stacy Ward and Candice Phipps; Jenna Williams and Helen Roberts.

And to Amy Hinkle, Lesley Morgan, Cari Levake, Taya Trent, Danny Sharp, Mindy Larew, and Laura Trent for their dedication since the Spring of 2015 when meetings began around a big square table in the "Nurse's Office," as well as Mary Marra, Deanna Garrett, Michelle Cheasty, Jerri Hinebaugh, Lucy Godwin, Julia Nestor, Felicia Pancoast; Ryan Deems, Leslie Shreve, Kristin Kroll, Meighan Carder, and Amy Reinhart, who piloted component work those first years of the new process. Also to the teachers that piloted the CTE Components as they rolled out: Tim Bode, Brianne McCauley, Trina Runner, and Julie Yearego.

Kudos to Jaimie Murphy who rocked the leprechaun lesson!

Thanks for the support of Dr. Carla Warren and Lorrie Smith, as well as Dr. Donna Hage and Dr. Mark Manchin; thanks to my friend, Anita.

For the support of T2: Heidi Griffith, Grant Spencer, Amy HInkle, Libby Jarom, and Eric Lemley.

To Andrea and Elizabeth—thank you for being my godly counsel in everything.

This book is dedicated to my son Derek, whom I love very much, and to my husband, Bill, who (thankfully) understands the love of projects.

Many thanks to God who is the giver of all good things, even ideas.

About the Author

Photo by Sam Santilli

Joetta Schneider first certified in AYA Science, Chemistry, in 2006, and renewed in 2016. She was a teacher of chemistry, biology, Earth science, environmental science, and general science for twenty-three years. She's certified in both AP Chemistry and Physics, as well. She served as a National Board assessor in 2008.

As a classroom teacher, she did all the normal things that teachers do, like teaching a full schedule while serving as advisor for the prom and sponsoring clubs. She was the Chair of the Science Department at her high school, and worked for ten years as an adjunct professor of Biology and Chemistry at a local university. Like most NBCTs, Joetta enjoys projects and learning new things.

In 2014, she became an Academic Coach, where part of her job included serving as a regional cohort facilitator for National Board candidates. This was a labor of love and a constant work in progress since the process for National Board Certification was revised, component-by-component, from 2013 to 2017. She now works with her friends, The Inklings, on the board of the Harrison County NBCT Facilitators and Friends, a non-profit organization which advocates for candidates and NBCTs in their local cohort.

Joetta is the CEO of JS Educational Consulting and Coaching.

Introduction

This book is intended to help teachers gain a broad overview of the entire National Board Certification process for teachers. Understanding the big picture helps candidates in their pursuit of the famous "a-ha moment." This course takes the approach that once teachers see the big picture, they can begin their work with more clarity and attend to the details of the process along the way.

It was originally written for teachers who decided to commit to National Board Certification and then had no idea how to start—because candidates often wonder where to start. However, FastTrack™ is also a great resource for any other teacher thinking about pursuing National Board Certification, or for a candidate who knows what to do but would like additional resources. This would be a great resource for teacher professional development, in general. For Districts wanting to use National Board certification as a platform or model for teacher professional development, the process—based on the work of the National Board of Professional Teaching Standards (NBPTS)—can be found at nbpts.org. The NBCTs on our team are available to present the program to your teachers.

In this book we walk you through mini experiences that help you gain skills or information to help you begin to piece together the big picture. You will need to attend to the details of each component, as well. We help you with that at times in the binder work. What this book cannot be is a guarantee that you will pass National Board certification if you use it, but you know that. This is another great resource at your disposal. Ultimately, your submission to the NBPTS must be "your own work." Thankfully, the National Board does not have a "cookie cutter" ideal of what an National Board Certified Teacher looks like, sounds like, or teaches like. If you meet the requirements you'll make it, and if you don't, you can refine your work until it meets the standards in the rubric.

How To Use This Book

1. Begin by using the candidate resources at the NBPTS.org website to determine the correct certificate area for you.

2. Then PRINT or DOWNLOAD all of the pages of Components 1-4. You will use these materials as you go through this workbook. Are you a person who likes to work with printed materials? Or will you be fine using a file downloaded on your computer? Candidates often make binders with tabs for each of the various components before beginning their candidacy.

3. Lastly, PRINT or DOWNLOAD the "General Portfolio Instructions" from the NBPTS website.

4. You will use all these materials throughout this course and throughout your candidacy.

5. There are blank pages inserted so you will have more room for writing; add additional pages as necessary.

6. You may find the Index or Explanation of Terms to be useful reading either before you start the course or as you go along.

7. Use the instructions and access codes at the back of this book to view the teaching videos associated with each chapter. These will help you develop your understanding of the concepts.

8. The process feels "vague" at first. This is normal. That is because you are building your understanding. Generally, you will have an a-ha moment around the time you complete one of your first components.

Key to Activity Icons

This icon indicates a journaling activity that will help you access experiences, thoughts, or ideas you already have.

The binder icon represents work you will use with materials you have downloaded from the nbpts.org website.

The video monitor represents material that is also presented in the companion videos to this book. Please look for the video access information on page 108 of this book.

This icon represents a short quiz so that you can check your understanding of the chapter topic.

When you see the notepad icon, you will be engaging in a writing exercise.

This icon will be found in the top corner of the keys to any quizzes.

Statement of Candidate Responsibility:

It is important that you understand that the work you submit to the National Board for Professional Teaching Standards must be your own work, and yours alone. The NBPTS has no "cookie cutter" ideal of what makes a National Board Certified Teacher, they do, however have criteria for teachers to meet that indicate they are accomplished teachers. These criteria are clearly listed in the level 4 rubric of each component.

My National Board is not affiliated with the NBPTS and we cannot guarantee that you will achieve your certification as a result of using our resources. However, we can guarantee that a thorough use of these resources will help you in your teaching, and we can state that we have facilitated many candidates on a one-one basis who have found this information useful.

It is important to note that achieving National Board certification is a developmental process—like walking or reading. You will have your personal timeline for success, and if you don't achieve as quickly as another candidate it does not mean you aren't as good a teacher. It means your mind is creating the synapses necessary for your own understanding and synthesis of the projects involved in certification.

In addition to the the FastTrack™ course, My National Board for Teachers provides workshops and one-to-one coaching for candidates. To find out more, go to our website, MyNationalBoard.com.

I understand that the work I submit to the NBPTS must be my work and mine alone, although collaboration with peers is fine and is also beneficial professional development.

_____

Candidate signature   date

Chapter 1 —

The Assessment Center

Your work at the assessment center will demonstrate that you know the second of the Five Core Propositions© of the National Board for Professional Teaching Standards (NBPTS), "Teachers know the subjects they teach and how to teach those subjects to students." This entry accounts for 40% of your total score.

Most teachers have had experience with subject matter examinations, so we spend more time in this chapter discussing how you demonstrate your content area pedagogy, which comes through most strongly in the constructed response items.

Under the old system, conventional wisdom was to take the assessment center test last— it was 100% essay questions back then and we thought it would be better to have internalized the standards so they would be automatic in our writing. In general, that approach worked. Some of the candidates on the new system have, indeed, ended up re-taking some of the test items when they take the Component 1 first. However, that's not the case across the board. About half our candidates don't have to retake any parts of the test although they've placed C1 first in their lineup. Lately, candidates on the new system are advising their peers to take Component 1 early in their candidacy, so they can easily fit it into their schedule to retake certain segments again if needed.

My advice would be to try the practice prompts before making your decision to see if you feel very familiar with the topics. Here's an example: an ELA candidate who had never taught writing. When she practiced the prompts, the writing portion didn't feel good to her. That was, indeed, the constructed response portion she ended up retaking. It worked out well for her because she had a whole year to learn to teach writing and borrowed a friend's class to do so.

The bottom line is that it is no longer necessary to wait to take C1 last if you would like to complete that component before you do others.

FastTrack™ Chapter 1

Activity 1

Activity 1.1— Thinking About Your Content

Directions: Respond to the following prompt:

What are some new initiatives or changes in the teaching of your content area?

Photo by William Stitt on Unsplash

Discussion of Activity 1.1 —

When you read your Standards, you will see that it is important that you are knowledgeable of new ideas in your content area. It is also important that, as a professional teacher, you decide how you feel about these new ideas once you've tried them. For example, if you have taught first grade for ten years and a new trend is "whole-brain-teaching," you do not have to use it. But you should realize that it's a trend right now for keeping students engaged. Other examples would be the "eight mathematical habits of mind" for math teaching, "proficiency over accuracy" for World Languages, or "Task Based Language Teaching." Other trends include: Makerspaces, Project-Based Learning, Teaching Empathy, and STEAM. Take some time to think about the current pedagogy for your certificate area, and if you aren't currently attending your certificate area conferences, spend time researching current trends and teaching techniques. Throughout this book you will find that I continually stress the importance of research to the National Board Certification process—because National Board Certified teachers aren't perfect teachers; they are good teachers with a growth mindset.

"National Board certified teachers aren't perfect teachers; they are good teachers with a growth mindset."

FastTrack™ Chapter 1

Activity 2

Activity 1.2— Understanding the Standards

Directions: Use the Standards you printed from NBPTS to complete the following activity. Hopefully you have at least skim-read your Standards once. Now you are reading them to prepare for your Component 1 Test. Because your Standards are probably close to 100 pages long, you should schedule an appropriate number of days to complete this activity.

Your content test will assess your understanding of these National Board Standards; they are very clear about what "accomplished teachers" of your certificate area know and do. Consider this quote from the Science Standards,

> "Accomplished teachers realize that the need for safety in science extends to all outside learning activities, including outdoor lessons, field trips, or independent home projects…" (1)

To apply this to a constructed response question for example, you would respond to a question about working with students in environments outside the classroom in order to meet an instructional goal by including the safety precautions needed. A careful examination of the NB Standards—in conjunction with your experience in your content area—will come through in an accomplished response to a question on the assessment.

Part I. Go through all of the pages of your standards and underline or highlight every instance that says, "Accomplished teachers..." or "For instance..." These are items that could occur in your constructed response questions about your classroom practice. It would be impossible for you to memorize all these instances, so don't try. Pay attention to the examples that you hadn't thought of or that are new to you.

Part II. Go back through the Standards one more time. This time look for buzz words or new ideas to research.

FastTrack™ Chapter 1

Activity 3

Activity 1.3— Your Content Knowledge

Part I. In the video we discussed ideas for preparing for the assessment center Component 1 by identifying your strengths and weaknesses.

1. What would you say are your content area strengths?

2. What content areas are your weakest?

3. Where can you get and practice the content information you need? (Examples: Khan Academy, CK-12, online Praxis tests…)

Part II. Use the internet to find other teachers on chat boards or Facebook pages, or other sites where teachers discuss ideas for increasing readiness and content area knowledge. There is a lot of information online, so while preparing for your Component 1, you may find it helpful to focus on discussion threads or information that specifically relate to Component 1. One way to sort the information is to search for hashtags, #C1 or #Component1.

Making a Plan to Study for the Content Test

1.   Which of the following resources will you use? (circle all that apply)

    a. Introductory college textbook for the course

    b. Praxis® study materials (including online practice tests)

    c. Online websites or apps such as Khan Academy or CK-12

    d. Text you teach from in your content area

    e. Streaming videos or DVDs about your certification area content

2. Look through the content and decide how many chapters you need to study, and how many weeks or months you have to do so. Divide the number of chapters by the number of weeks you have to prepare.

> Example: If there are 18 chapters in your introductory Science course, and you have 36 weeks till the test, you will have two weeks to study each chapter.

3. Search through the NBPTS Standards in your certificate area for content area topics: do you see that Geometry teachers must teach reflections, for example? Do your Art Standards mention that art teachers teach art criticism? Do Literacy Standards say that you are competent in teaching listening skills? Make a list of the content competencies in your Standards.

FastTrack™ Chapter 1

Activity 4

Activity 1.4— Assessment Center Practice

Thinking and composing ideas quickly will help you with the timed test at the assessment center. In your Component 1 information from NBPTS, you have several practice questions. Find a quiet place where you can work without distractions and complete the following activity.

Copy and paste one of the practice questions into an open Word document and set a timer for 30 minutes. Now compose and proofread your answer, stopping only when your time is up.

Compare your answer with the Level 4 Rubric found in your Component 1 Instructions. It may be helpful to have another teacher in your content area look at the instructions, prompt, and rubric, as well as your answer, to give you feedback about the strengths and weaknesses in your work. This is a great time for the informal professional development you will have in discussing teaching with another teacher in your content area!

Complete this activity with each of the practice questions available to you. Remember to discuss the answers with other teachers in your content area—the questions will vary some from those at the assessment center, but this is a chance to deepen your understanding and perspective about your content.

Notes

FastTrack™ Chapter 1

Activity 5

Activity 1.5— Quiz on Content Knowledge

1. Good methods for studying for the content knowledge assessment would be:

   A. Practicing with online content sites such as Khan Academy

   B. Studying from course texts with the same content as your certification area

   C. Studying the standards that will be assessed on this entry

   D. Practicing with the prompts given in the NBPTS instructions

   E. All of the above

2. The content knowledge that is preferred for National Board certification:

   A. Is one grade level higher than the developmental level you will certify in

   B. Is the knowledge a teacher would have after teaching the content for more than three years

   C. Includes knowledge of how to address student misconceptions

   D. More than one of these is correct

   E. None of the above

3. From the level 4 rubric, one key to receiving an exemplary score on constructed response items is:

    A. Mentioning formative assessment strategies in your response

    B. Utilizing information from the textbook

    C. Evidence that is clear, consistent, and convincing

    D. Understanding student dispositions

    E. All of the above

4. A link to the online assessment tutorial can be found at:

    A. The Praxis website

    B. The Assessment Center Testing page

    C. The My National Board Facebook page

    D. Any local community college site

    E. All of the above

5. Candidates that score well on the Component 1 test:

    A. Are teachers who have mastered the GRE

    B. Are teachers who are well-versed in the pedagogy of their field

    C. Are teachers who write about diagnostic assessment in their constructed response items

    D. Are teachers who test in the top 10% of all candidates

    E. None of the above

FastTrack™ Chapter 1

Activity 5

Key to Activity 1.5— Quiz on Content Knowledge

1. Good methods for studying for the content knowledge assessment would be:

    A. Practicing with online content sites such as Khan Academy

    B. Studying from course texts with the same content as your certification area

    C. Studying the standards that will be assessed on this entry

    D. Practicing with the prompts given in the NBPTS instructions

    E. <u>All of the above</u>

2. The content knowledge that is preferred for National Board certification:

    A. Is one grade level higher than the developmental level you will certify in

    B. Is the knowledge a teacher would have after teaching the content for more than three years

    C. Includes knowledge of how to address student misconceptions

    D. <u>More than one of these is correct *B&C</u>

    E. None of the above

3. From the level 4 rubric, one key to receiving an exemplary score on constructed response items is:

   A. Mentioning formative assessment strategies in your response

   B. Utilizing information from the textbook

   C. <u>Evidence that is clear, consistent, and convincing</u>

   D. Understanding student dispositions

   E. All of the above

4. A link to the online assessment tutorial can be found at:

   A. The Praxis website

   B. <u>The Assessment Center Testing page</u>

   C. The My National Board Facebook page

   D. Any local community college site

   E. All of the above

5. Candidates that score well on the Component 1 test:

   A. Are teachers who have mastered the GRE

   B. <u>Are teachers who are well-versed in the pedagogy of their field</u>

   C. Are teachers who write about diagnostic assessment in their constructed response items

   D. Are teachers who test in the top 10% of all candidates

   E. None of the above

Chapter 2—

Planning, Teaching, and Learning

In this component, you choose a sequence of instruction to showcase how you plan and implement your lessons, as well as your ability to differentiate instruction for students. You also analyze student work samples to determine the impact of your teaching on student learning. This aligns with the National Board for Professional Teaching Standards' Propositions numbers one and three: "Teachers are committed to students and their learning," and "Teachers are responsible for managing and monitoring student learning."

It will be important for you to use your NBPTS instructions to make good choices in your sequence of instruction and in the students you choose to feature. Beyond that, the "big picture" for this component is that you will choose goals appropriate to your students and your teaching context, plan the sequence of instruction—including differentiation for students you think may have trouble reaching the learning goals, teach the "unit," and then analyze the work of students to determine the impact of your teaching. Component 2 requires that you understand the Architecture of Accomplished Teaching© of the NBPTS. Your score on this entry will be 15% of your overall score.

In this chapter, one of our primary goals is to understand differentiation of instruction for the purpose of serving students individually, as well as differentiating instruction for your class as a whole.

FastTrack™ Chapter 2

Activity 1

Activity 2.1— Planning for Accomplished Teaching

Directions: Respond to the following prompts; then look at examples of answers to this section in the video.

1. Describe a lesson that worked well with one group of students but did not work with a different group of students OR describe a time you changed a lesson to better suit your students.

2. Try to list twenty ways a teacher can know about students as learners or as individuals.

3. Describe a time when your knowledge of a student helped you teach that student more effectively.

FastTrack™ Chapter 2

Activity 2

Activity 2.2— Deconstructing Component 2 Instructions

Directions: Use the Component 2 materials you printed from NBPTS to answer the following questions.

Part I. Use the "Overview" section to fill in the blanks, below.

- "List: "details this entry provides you the opportunity to…"

_____

_____

_____

- What is the overall focus of this entry and rubrics?

_____

_____

_____

_____

- Which instructions are specific to your certificate area that are in the Overview? (for example, music teachers must provide videos, but other areas don't.)

_____

_____

_____

_____

_____

_____

_____

- List the Standards on which your work will be evaluated in this entry:

_____

_____

_____

_____

Q: Who is Eligible for Board Certification?

A: Candidates must possess a bachelor's degree, a valid state teaching license, and three years of classroom or school counselor experience prior to starting the certification process. (NOTE: Candidates for the Career and Technical Education certificate are required to hold a bachelor's degree only if their state required one for their current license).

— nbpts.org FAQ

Directions: Use the Component 2 materials from NBPTS to answer the following questions.

Part II. Complete the following sentences in the section, "What Do I Need To Do?"

- "In this entry you demonstrate…"

_____

_____

_____

_____

- "You provide evidence of…"

_____

_____

_____

_____

- "You analyze and assess…"

_____

_____

_____

_____

- "In this entry you submit…" (five things)

_____

_____

_____

_____

_____

_____

_____

_____

_____

_____

_____

_____

Part III. Under the section titled, "What Do I Need to Submit?"

    A. How many pages are allowed for each of the following?

        1. Your contextual information sheet

        2. Your written commentary

        3. Instructional Activities materials

        4. Student work samples

        5. Culminating Assessment

        6. Other

    B. Is there a timeframe for your sequence of instruction, and if so, what is it?

    C. Look for instructions that tell you how to select the lessons and instruction you are to feature. These are very certificate specific. Read and highlight any instructions that tell you how to choose the correct lessons for this entry.

D. What directions are given to you regarding how to choose the student(s) you will be working with?

E. Is there anything you are NOT allowed to do when choosing the students or the activities? (For example, do you have to use different students for Components 2 and 3?)

Part IV. Answer the following reflection question.

What content and topics are you thinking (right now) might work for this?

Part V. Skip ahead to the section titled, "Composing Your Written Commentary."

Write a short answer to the first question in each section (they are bulleted in yellow.) You are just practicing so don't worry about perfection—use the unit of instruction you are currently teaching to get a feel for the writing you need to do. The key is to get something down on paper to start.

1. Instructional Context—

2. Planning Instruction—

3. Analysis of Instruction and Student Work—

4. Reflection—

FastTrack™ Chapter 2

Activity 3

Activity 2.3— Accomplished Lesson Planning

For this activity, you will be using the GENERAL PORTFOLIO INSTRUCTIONS for Components 2,3, and 4, which are found on the nbpts.org website under "Resources," then "First Time and Returning Candidates," and then scrolling down two small sections to "Instructions."

(Begin on page 6.)

   1. List the five core propositions of the National Board: (You may shorten them.)

A. _____

B. _____

C. _____

D. _____

E. _____

Hint: In the future, when you write about your teaching, remember that the 5-Core Propositions should be evident in your work—they are the philosophy from which the standards and all other work stems.

2.   List the 6 closely linked stages that make up accomplished teaching on the Architecture of Accomplished Teaching© helix.

FastTrack™ Chapter 2

Activity 4

Activity 2.4— Differentiated Instruction

Part I. In the video we saw four ways to differentiate. List them here:

1. _____

An example of when I have done this is:

2. _____

An example of when I have done this is:

3. _____

An example of when I have done this is:

4. _____

An example of when I have done this is:

What is Differentiated Instruction?

First, let's make the distinction between differentiation OF instruction and differentiation FOR instruction. When you try to use different teaching strategies, formats, or approaches rather than "just lecture all the time," for example, then you are differentiating your methods of instruction. When you are choosing methods of instruction to meet the needs of specific learners in your classroom, you are differentiating FOR instruction of those students. In Component 2, the NBPTS asks you to demonstrate your ability to differentiate instruction to meet the needs of your students, including your featured students.

Differentiated Instruction (DI) has its roots in Multiple Intelligences theory by Howard Gardner. The idea is that different students have different strengths and different "best ways" to learn. The idea was the subject of several books by Carol Ann Tomlinson, a leading proponent of DI. [1]

The key to differentiating instruction is to know and understand your students. Such relational teaching is effective in understanding a student's strengths and motivations. This type of teaching is especially effective because motivated students have a feeling of efficacy and optimism toward learning—they begin to think "I can do this." Teachers who understand their students help students learn by making learning accessible. Teachers actively plan for student differences so that all students can learn.[2]

> "Successful differentiation depends on knowing your students as human beings and as learners."

What Are Some Examples of DI?

Some ways to differentiate instruction include differentiating the process, the content, the product, and the learning environment.[3] For example: a science teacher may realize that a student who is a baseball player could relate to the weight of a baseball bat when converting pounds or ounces to grams and use this idea to overcome his aversion to the math of metric conversions. The teacher already knew her student had an aversion to math and proactively chose some examples to make learning more accessible. By using example problems relevant to a learner, the teacher gives a student context that helps him or her learn.

An example of differentiating the product might be allowing students the choice of turning in an essay or a PowerPoint as his or her summative assessment, or allowing students to prepare an iMovie presentation rather than present in front of the class. When a teacher understands a student's social anxiety and allows the student to prepare this presentation at home for his classmates, this is also an example of differentiation of the learning environment.

When a social studies teacher knows that a student struggles to read, he might assign current event reading using Newsela—online software that can adapt the reading level of a news article for each learner. This is especially effective when students in the class are unaware that they are all reading the same article at different reading levels. Using technology is one way to differentiate instruction. In this case, the teacher differentiates the content for specific students.

Differentiation of instruction is usually done proactively. When you are writing about planning, you will be asked about how you planned for differentiation. An added bonus in differentiating for students is that this can only be done successfully by your engaging with them during the learning process. This engagement with your students will also help you to formatively assess and adjust during the instruction.

What are Some Non-Examples?

Some non-examples of differentiation include: having advanced students teach struggling students, not giving homework to advanced students, grouping students according to ability, giving advanced students more free time, and allowing students to choose their own books from a list.[4] Differentiation is also not "IEPs for all students." The key to differentiation of instruction is knowing your students as people; it's a relational endeavor. Think about when someone who knows you well can help you understand a concept. This is what a teacher does when she differentiates to help kids understand. It's the heart of the famous saying, "I don't teach content, I teach students."

What are Some Best Practices in Differentiation?

Take the time to get to know your students throughout the year. You can start a binder or notebook, or some kind of file where you can record information about the students in your class to review whenever you need to—perhaps before each new grading period. Your genuine curiosity about each student will make differentiation easier.

Research differentiation practices. A key characteristic of a National Board Certified Teacher (NBCT) is that he or she is a lifelong learner. There is a high probability of many new strategies and ideas in education each year—and you want to demonstrate that you are up-to-date with current research that helps you make an impact on your students.

What are Some Other Benefits of Differentiation?

Knowing your students and differentiating for them will also help you with classroom management. Students seek connection with you and their peers. When you demonstrate genuine caring and concern for them, they are more apt to listen to you. Additionally, when learning and doing well are perceived as possible, fewer students will "check out." One side effect of differentiation is better classroom management when you proactively think about how to impact student learning through knowledge of your students.

References and Resources

1. http://www.caroltomlinson.com/books.html\

2. http://www.ascd.org/research-a-topic/differentiated-instruction-resources.aspx

3. https://www.teachthought.com/pedagogy/what-is-differentiated-instruction/

4. https://www.edutopia.org/blogs/tag/differentiated-instruction

5. https://www.prodigygame.com/blog/differentiated-instruction-strategies-examples-download/

6. Sense*Able* Strategies—Including Diverse Learners Through Multisensory Strategies, Anne M. Beninghof, 1998, published by Sophis West Educational Services.

Photo by laith abuabdu on

FastTrack™ Chapter 2

Activity 5

Activity 2.5— Quiz on Differentiated Instruction

1. Differentiated instruction begins with:

A. Formative assessment

B. Diagnostic assessment

C. Knowledge of students

D. Activity ideas

E. None of the above

2. The parts of a lesson a teacher can differentiate are:

A. The instructional process

B. The products of the learning

C. The level or amount of content

D. The learning environment

E. All of the above

3. If a teacher wants to differentiate a lesson for particular students:

A. She can design group work that pairs high level students with struggling students

B. She can basically develop an IEP for each student

C. She can plan to provide supports she knows to be effective for particular students

D. She can ask the student to sit in a preferred seating section

E. All of the above

4. Which of the following is an appropriate differentiation strategy?

A. Providing the class with a list of helpful websites

B. Allowing students to choose where they sit as they work

C. Having extra time allowed for a lesson that may run long

D. Giving students information about tutoring services

E. All of the above

5. An added benefit of differentiation of instruction for students is:

A. Better classroom management

B. Better access to information

C. Fewer disruptions from the office

D. Improved learning goals

E. All of the above

FastTrack™ Chapter 2

Activity 5

Key to Activity 2.5— Quiz on Differentiated Instruction

1. Differentiated instruction begins with:

A. Formative assessment

B. Diagnostic assessment

C. <u>Knowledge of students</u>

D. Activity ideas

E. None of the above

2. The parts of a lesson a teacher can differentiate are:

A. The instructional process

B. The products of the learning

C. The level or amount of content

D. The learning environment

E. <u>All of the above</u>

3. If a teacher wants to differentiate a lesson for particular students:

A. She can design group work that pairs high level students with struggling students

B. She can basically develop an IEP for each student

C. <u>She can plan to provide supports she knows to be effective for particular students</u>

D. She can ask the student to sit in a preferred seating section

E. All of the above

4. Which of the following is an appropriate differentiation strategy?

A. Providing the class with a list of helpful websites

B. <u>Allowing students to choose where they sit as they work</u>

C. Having extra time allowed for a lesson that may run long

D. Giving students information about tutoring services

E. All of the above

5. An added benefit of differentiation of instruction for students is:

A. <u>Better classroom management</u>

B. Better access to information

C. Fewer disruptions from the office

D. Improved learning goals

E. All of the above

Chapter 3—

Evidence of Student Engagement

Your work in this chapter is to provide two videos that allow assessors to understand your ability to engage students in learning the content. You will also demonstrate your safe, equitable, and challenging learning environment, and your teaching methods in several different lesson formats. These ideas align with propositions one, two, and three of the Five Core Propositions© of the NBPTS. By understanding how to engage your students, you will be demonstrating your commitment to their learning. By understanding sound pedagogy that leads to student engagement, you will demonstrate that you know how to teach your content; finally, by fully engaging your students in learning the content, you will be actively managing and monitoring student learning. No wonder this component is worth 30% of your total score!

It can be difficult to get a good video. Therefore, strive to record lessons early and often. In our cohort, I like to have candidates bring in a first video to analyze in October. I won't go into it here, but you can find information about the timelines associated with National Board certification on our blog at mynationalboard.com.

In this chapter, you will learn what student engagement is and is not, as well as resources for learning some student engagement strategies. You will also consider how effective feedback helps to provide a safe, equitable, and challenging learning environment for students.

FastTrack™ Chapter 3

Activity 1

Activity 3.1— Envisioning Accomplished Teaching

Directions: Respond to the following prompts.

1. Remember one of your best teaching moments:

  • What was the content?

  • What was the lesson?

  • What were you doing?

  • What were the students doing?

  • How did you know the students were learning?

- How did you prepare for that lesson?

- Were there special efforts you took to make that lesson happen, or special resources you found?

- How many times have you taught that lesson?

2. Describe a great lesson or learning activity that impacted you as a student.

3. Imagine that you walk into the classroom of a great teacher teaching a great lesson! What would you hear, see, and feel?

FastTrack™ Chapter 3

Activity 2

Activity 3.2— Deconstructing Your Component 3 Instructions

Directions: Use the Component 3 materials from NBPTS website to complete the following activities and questions.

Part I. Use the "Overview" section to fill in the blanks, below.

List: "details this entry captures details of…"

_____

_____

_____

_____

_____

_____

_____

_____

_____

_____

What is the evidence on which you will be evaluated?

_____

_____

_____

_____

How many videos will you need to submit, and how long should they be?

_____

_____

_____

_____

List the Standards that your work will be evaluated on in this entry:

_____

_____

_____

_____

Part II. Complete the following sentences in the section, "What Do I Need To Do?"

"This entry captures your ability to…"

_____

_____

_____

_____

"The videos you submit should show…"

_____

_____

_____

_____

"Together the two lessons must…"

_____

_____

_____

_____

"In this entry you…"

- describe

_____

_____

_____

_____

_____

_____

_____

- demonstrate

_____

_____

_____

_____

_____

- provide

_____

_____

_____

_____

_____

_____

_____

- explain

_____

_____

_____

_____

_____

_____

Part III. Find the section titled, "Recording Your Videos."

A. Highlight the sentence that begins: "It is important that you…"

B. Highlight the important words in each of the statements preceded by square yellow bullets given under "Follow the guidelines…"

       Here's an example:

   "<u>If you do not receive permission to include a student or adult</u> in a video, you must <u>ensure that he/she is out of</u>   <u>the camera's range and not heard</u>."

C. In the section titled, "Selecting The Class," what percentage of the class must fall within the age guidelines for your certificate? _____

D. The focus (of the video) is on your _____ and

_____

E. From the section, "Selecting A Lesson," the NBPTS says that students

should be able to _____, and that you promote their

learning by using

_____

_____

_____

Part IV. Answer the following reflection question.

Which lessons are you considering using for your Component 3 Videos?

Notes

FastTrack™ Chapter 3

Activity 3

Activity 3.3— Learning About Student Engagement

What Do You Know Already?

So far in chapter 3, you've thought about your own experiences with engaging lessons.

However, with National Board certification, you have an opportunity to grow in your understanding of your teaching, and this is why candidates often say it's the best professional development they've ever done.

Since Component 3 is about student engagement, let's spend some time solidifying that concept and even investigating it some.

Take a moment to pause the video and answer these two questions.

1. In one or two sentences, how would you define student engagement?

2. In your experience, what are the benefits of student engagement?

Why Should I Learn More About Student Engagement?

The many definitions of student engagement indicate that it's happening when students are invested in the tasks that they are completing in the classroom. It's important—and the time you spend researching and learning more about how to engage students in the classroom is important, too. Students who are engaged are highly motivated.

It will also add to your chances of success on Component 3. Accomplished teachers know how to engage students in learning the content of their class.

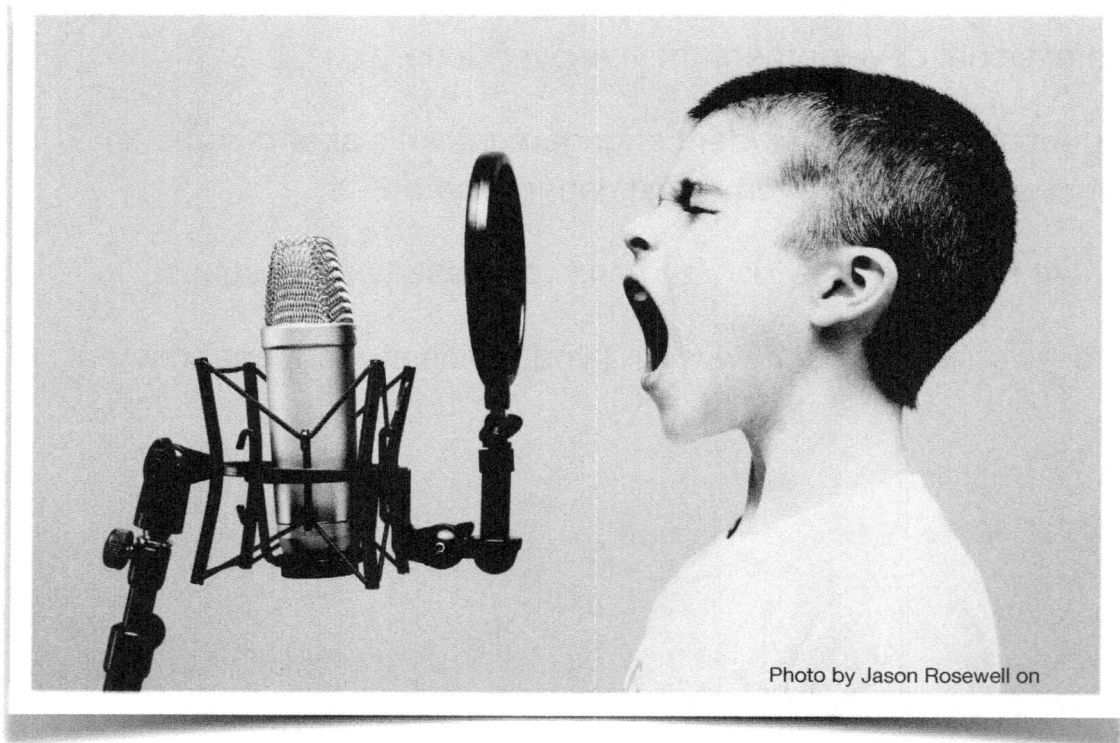

Photo by Jason Rosewell on

Some researchers have even developed a continuum of student engagement levels starting with authentic engagement and ending with actual rebellion.[3] Hopefully you have students at the top of the spectrum, authentically engaged, at least much of the time. Typically, teachers also have lessons on certain days or during certain moments in teaching when student levels of engagement could simply be described as "compliant." When my students are answering my questions or completing tasks I've asked them to complete, they are compliant, even if they seem to be doing the tasks with a good attitude.

Strive for your Component 3 videos to reach the realm of authentic engagement, as evidenced by student learning conversations.[4]

What is Student Engagement?

Authentic engagement of students with the content is identified by their willingness to work to solve a problem or produce a product—the sense that the student is invested in the outcome of the learning and not just going through the motions. When students are excited about the possibilities inherent in the learning, you will begin to hear student learning conversations that transcend the routine and extend into high level of engagement with ideas. Compare the following two statements by students learning about nanoparticles:

Student 1: "Ferrofluids spike because the nanoparticles in them have enough force to overcome the effects of gravity."

Student 2: "Whoa! I wonder how ferrofluids can be used on the moon? I think since there is less gravitational pull, ferrofluids would spike more than they do on earth."

Student #2 wants to know more about the behavior of ferrofluids and poses ideas that haven't been thought of (yet) by the teacher. Authentic student engagement can be a challenge for teachers to manage and sometimes we shy away from that. You may choose to record some "tried and true" lessons that you know are high interest for students, or you may end up redesigning some old lessons that you've always wanted to redesign. Maybe you'll end up starting from scratch. This is why your students will have the best teacher the year(s) you are engrossed in this process. If you ever wanted to prioritize and focus on your teaching and be the best teacher you can be, this process gives you a great opportunity for it.

Here is an example of a lesson designed to engage students in thinking about a concept. Two students are sorting through cards with objects of different sizes in as they begin a unit about the metric system:

Student #1 "The whale, then the ship. Wait, is a whale smaller or larger than a ship?"

Student #2 "I'm sure ships are bigger than whales. Well, actually, I'm not sure. Let's look that up."

Most teachers I know are glad when students want to look up answers to questions. Is the size of a ship vs. a whale relevant to students? Possibly— some of them have been to the ocean or on ships. Some students have been to aquariums and have seen whales. Maybe your students just enjoy animals.

How Can We Help Students Engage with the Content?

Looking at the questions in the "Written Commentary" section of your Component 3 Instructions, do any of them ask "what strategies did you use?"

It can be as simple as a challenge: "How many different ways can you multiply two numbers to get 48?"

For a language arts lesson, consider two second grade classrooms. In one classroom, the students are in their desks and the teacher asks students what they know about leprechauns. Students raise their hands and the teacher chooses three students to give their answers. She then tells the class to think about how they would catch a leprechaun. She waits one minute and then gives instructions for writing a story about catching a leprechaun. She has an outline on the board for students to reference as they are writing.

In another classroom, students are sitting on a carpet in whole group while the teacher shows a 3-minute video clip about how a boy is trying to catch a leprechaun, but the leprechaun escapes. She asks the students to think about how they would catch a leprechaun while she times them for one minute. She then tells them to turn to their partner and tell their partner how they would catch a leprechaun. After students spend 5-6 minutes talking, she has them go to their desks to begin writing their story. She has an outline on the board for them to follow as they begin writing.

Analyzing the Student Engagement in These Two Scenarios:

Think back to Teacher #1 — what strategies did she use to engage her students in writing the story? She might write that she asked questions to help students focus on the topic and provided time for them to think about the question before they began writing, or that she provided an outline on the board to help students build their story with a topic title, an introduction sentence, etc.

Teacher #2 might say she used a video clip to get students excited and thinking creatively; that she used the "Think-Pair-Share" strategy to help students verbalize their ideas before they wrote them down. She could write that she used movement between different sections of the activity to increase student engagement.[2,3] Then she would also add that she provided an outline on the board to help students build their story. It is important to note that neither of these teachers is "incorrect."

Why Is Student Engagement Important?

Let's take a step backward. Why do we want engaged students?

- The research is clear that there is a link to student achievement when students are engaged — students are motivated.[1,4,5]

- Student engagement results in better classroom behavior. [4]

- Engaged students are less likely to drop out of school.[7]

If you've been teaching any time at all, you know that it's a miserable day when you seem to be "pulling teeth" to get students to do what you want them to do. This is a simple indication that they aren't engaged in their tasks. Or maybe they're goofing off, or looking around. Maybe they're sleeping. Some teachers rationalize, "He works at night, he needs to sleep." I once heard a teacher say, "He's gifted and bored so I let him sleep." My thought is, you know your students, and depending on the viewpoint of your Principal, that might be okay for whatever reasons. But it's not the evidence of accomplished teaching that you want to showcase in your video. Send in the best video you can—one that showcases the students engaging with the content and with each other.

Self-Awareness Exercise:

Have you ever experienced actual rebellion from students? As a classroom teacher for 23 years, I can say that I have been guilty of lesson design and classroom management that led to disengagement at times and even in one or two cases, actual rebellion. Sometimes a student's rebellion is an attempt to gain their parent's attention. However, if you see evidence of these things in your classroom, please do not ignore those signs that your lesson planning and classroom management style may need work. Many National Board candidates are interested in becoming better teachers but don't take the time to do so. I will paraphrase here, but one of the questions an assessor will be asking themselves as they view your video and read your reflection is, "Does the teacher seem aware of the truth about his or her classroom?"

No judgment and no guilt. National Board Certified Teachers are not perfect teachers; they are good teachers with a growth mindset. If you and I have moments that aren't our best, that's part of our growth. Your assessors will be deciding whether the evidence you submit represents evidence of accomplished teaching. They will not be judging you as a teacher.

Now is a great time to learn new skills or, if you are already highly skilled at engaging your students, it's time to put your best foot forward!

How Can I Increase Student Engagement in My Classroom?

Tip #1 — Think in terms of authentic tasks or content that is relevant to students. When we ask elementary students to decide what the best ratio is for sugar to iced tea, we can teach ratios and solubility; we reach Bloom's Taxonomy levels of critical thinking and higher Depth of Knowledge. Students are engaged when they get to predict and test their ideas and when they get to explain their ideas to others. Project-based and problem based learning are lesson designs that can promote engagement when properly structured and scaffolded.[6]

Think about this project you are doing, National Board Certification, and how self-motivated you are as you are completing it! It's a perfect example of authentic interest. No one made you do this. Engaged learners are optimistic! You are passionate about teaching and learning! You are curious about the growth experience you've been offered, and consumed with thoughts about how to achieve your goals!

Think about other times you've gone online to find more information or taken classes to learn something on your own. This is how you want your students to feel about the lessons you design. Not every lesson will result in passion from your students. But the ones you video record for your Component 3 will need to be at these higher levels of engagement.

Tip #2— If you haven't already had training in this, spend a few hours researching strategies for increasing student engagement. Use the resources I've listed at the end of this chapter. Try a few of them before the lesson you're actually hoping to use. You are looking for student engagement with each other and with the content. For example, we can tell that students are thinking about the content and are learning from each other in the following conversation:

> Student 1: "Do you think I should draw Doric columns or Corinthian columns?"
>
> Student 2: "Could we have Ionic columns on the poster?"
>
> Student 1: "Sure, they were a part of Greek Architecture, too!"

Tip #3— If you have some "tried and true" lessons, for example, if you were a math teacher and had taught a lesson with "Barbie Bungee Jumping" that always get students engaged in predicting, observing, and explaining the math content, you might start there. You might plan for opportunities to record five or six lessons so you have plenty of video footage to choose from.

Questions for Reflection:

- How can you design lessons that engage students at the level of curiosity, interest, passion, persistence, and even wonder?

- How well do you design lessons that earn a student's attention and commitment to learn?

References and Resources

1. Research Proof Points—Better Student Engagement Improves Student Learning

https://www.nwea.org/blog/2015/research-proof-points-better-student-engagement-improves-student-learning/

2. The Glossary of Education Reform definition of student engagement

http://edglossary.org/student-engagement/

3. Seven Ways to Increase Student Engagement in the Classroom

https://www.readinghorizons.com/blog/seven-ways-to-increase-student-engagement-in-the-classroom

4. Tips from Dr. Marzano, author of *The Highly Engaged Classroom*

https://www.marzanoresearch.com/resources/tips/hec_tips_archive

5. The Eight C's of Engagement

http://lackawannaschools.org/cms/lib/NY19000337/Centricity/ModuleInstance/865/TheEight_Cs_of_Engagement.pdf

6. Student Engagement

https://soundout.org/defining-student-engagement-a-literature-review/

7. NM Innovation Zone Journey

http://nminnovationzone.blogspot.com/2011/

8. National Dropout Prevention Center

http://dropoutprevention.org/ndpcn-headlines/national-dropout-prevention-centernetwork-releases-position-paper-identifying-importance-of-student-engagement-in-reducing-dropout-rates/

"Think about this project you are doing, National Board certification, and how self-motivated you are as you are completing it! It's a perfect example of authentic interest."

FastTrack™ Chapter 3.

Activity 4

Activity 3.4— Thinking About Feedback to Students

Directions: Reflect on the following statements.

1. "Feedback is not advice, praise, or evaluation. Feedback is information about how one is doing in effort to reach a goal."[1]

2. "Feedback should be specific, immediate, and—in the best cases— involves the learner in the process. Feedback should not be judgmental or negative."

3. What are some ways that you have given feedback to students that has helped move them forward in their understanding?

4. What have you read in your Standards about giving feedback to students?

FastTrack™ Chapter 3

Activity 5

Activity 3.5— Quiz on Student Engagement

1. Student engagement is evident when students:

A. Pay attention to the lesson

B. Are invested in the learning

C. Are passionate about learning

D. Are curious about the lesson

E. All of the above

2. A benefit of student engagement mentioned in the video is:

A. Fewer fights on the playground

B. Increased student ownership of grades

C. Increased motivation

D. Higher test scores

E. None of the above

3. If a teacher wants to increase student engagement, he could try:

A. Increasing the amount of homework for unengaged students

B. Increasing his own understanding of teaching strategies

C. Decreasing the number of paragraphs students write daily

D. Decreasing the number of worksheets each class period

E. All of the above

4. Which of the following lesson designs is most likely to be engaging:

A. Lessons that are project-based or problem-based

B. Lessons that are perceived as relevant to their lives

C. Lessons that involve higher levels of Bloom's Taxonomy

D. Lessons that allow for student learning conversations

E. All of the above

5. In your Component 3 videos, we should be able to see evidence that:

A. Your classroom is a safe and challenging environment

B. You have listed your content objectives for students and parents

C. Your National Board candidate ID number is on the board

D. Students are engaged in Socratic thinking

E. None of the above

FastTrack™ Chapter 3

Activity 5

Key to Activity 3.5— Quiz on Student Engagement

1. Student engagement is evident when students:

A. Pay attention to the lesson

B. Are invested in the learning

C. Are passionate about learning

D. Are curious about the lesson

E. <u>All of the above</u>

2. A benefit of student engagement mentioned in the video is:

A. Fewer fights on the playground

B. Increased student ownership of grades

C. <u>Increased motivation</u>

D. Higher test scores

E. None of the above

3. If a teacher wants to increase student engagement, he could try:

A.   Increasing the amount of homework for unengaged students

B.   <u>Increasing his own understanding of teaching strategies</u>

C.   Decreasing the number of paragraphs students write daily

D.   Decreasing the number of worksheets each class period

E.   All of the above

4. Which of the following lesson designs is most likely to be engaging:

A.   Lessons that are project-based or problem-based

B.   Lessons that are perceived as relevant to their lives

C.   Lessons that involve higher levels of Bloom's Taxonomy

D.   Lessons that allow for student learning conversations

E.   <u>All of the above</u>

5. In your Component 3 videos, we should be able to see evidence that:

A.   <u>Your classroom is a safe and challenging environment</u>

B.   You have listed your content objectives for students and parents

C.   Your National Board candidate ID number is on the board

D.   Students are engaged in Socratic thinking

E.   None of the above

Takeaways—

- Do your research on ways to increase student engagement
- Practice some strategies and think about some you already use.
- Strive for high levels of student engagement with content and with each other

Chapter 4 —

Reflecting on the Development of Your Practice

Component 4 is a broader look at your practice, and the experience you've gained through the years will be evidenced by your work with current students. It's based in propositions four and five of the Five Core Propositions — "Teachers think systematically about their practice and learn from experience," and "Teachers are members of learning communities."

At first glance this component seems similar to the work you did for Component 2; however, in this work, you will take a wider view of your teaching practice as a whole and compare it to the Architecture of Accomplished Teaching® as established by the NBPTS. Unlike C2, this entry is more about your teaching practice or career than about one unit of instruction. Component 4 is worth 15% of your total score.

This chapter includes information on formative and summative assessment, diagnostic assessment (as one type of formative assessment,) and student self-assessment. It also discusses helping students learn how they learn. When you are able to help students OWN their learning, you are on the right track. Don't forget to show measurable impact on student learning.

An experienced, professional teacher will tell you his or her practice didn't get this accomplished in a vacuum, and in this chapter, you look at the two-way communication and collaboration you have with parents, other professionals, and/or community members.

Altogether we will see how you have worked as a learner, leader, and/or collaborator to impact student learning and advocate for student needs.

FastTrack™ Chapter 4

Activity 1

Activity 4.1— Thinking About Your Practice

Directions: Respond to the following prompt:

Describe a spiral in your work with students that looks somewhat like this:

1) I know about _this_ overarching need of a group of students, from information I've gathered from a variety of sources. _This_ is the data I used to create the student profile.

2) And because of _this_ need, I have advocated with other professionals for _this way of addressing the student need_. _This is the data_ showing the impact the work of our collaborative community had on the group of students..

3) Because of what I know about these students, it has affected my assessment of students _this way_.

Formative Assessment:

Student Self-Assessment:

Summative Assessment:

Here is the data from those assessments:

4) In the process of addressing the student need, I— and possibly with others— found that there was a need for _this_ professional development, in which I fulfilled this role of leader, learner, and/or collaborator to attain or provide that professional development. And _this data_ shows the impact it had on students.

Fast Track™ Chapter 4

Activity 2

Activity 4.2— Deconstructing Your Component 4 Instructions

Directions: Use the Component 4 materials you printed from NBPTS to complete the following activities.

Part I. Use the "Overview" section to fill in the blanks, below.

- How does this entry provide you "the opportunity to highlight your abilities as an effective and reflective practitioner?"

_____

_____

_____

_____

_____

_____

_____

_____

- "your group consists of …"

- "use assessments to…"

- "and provide evidence of…"

_____

_____

_____

_____

_____

_____

"…and of your contributions to…"

_____

_____

_____

_____

_____

_____

_____

_____

Directions: Use the Component 4 materials from NBPTS to answer the following questions.

Part II. List the Standards on which this submission will be evaluated:

_____

_____

_____

_____

_____

Part III. Complete the following sentences in the section, "What Do I Need To Do?"

- "You demonstrate…"

_____

_____

_____

_____

_____

_____

- "You use your knowledge…"

_____

_____

_____

_____

_____

_____

- "In this entry you reflect…"

_____

_____

_____

_____

_____

_____

Part III. Under the section titled, "What Do I Need to Submit?"

A. How many pages are allowed for each of the following?

    1. Your Contextual Information Sheet

    2. Your Group Information and Profile Form

    3. Generation and Use of Assessment Data:

        (1) Instructional Context Form

        (2) Formative Assessment Form

        (3) Associated Evidence

        (4) Student Self-Assessment

        (5) Summative Assessment Form

        (6) The Summative Assessment or Description of It

        (7) Results of the Assessment

    4. Participation in Learning Communities

        (1) Description of the Professional Learning Need

        (2) Associated Evidence

        (3) Description of Student Need

        (4) Associated Evidence

    5. Written Commentary

B. Is there a time frame for your sequence of instruction, and if so, what is it?

C. What directions are given to you regarding how to choose the student(s) you will be working with?

D. Is there anything you are NOT allowed to do when choosing the students or the activities? (For example, do you have to use different activities for Components 2 and 4?)

FastTrack™ Chapter 4

Activity 3

Activity 4.3— Understanding Assessment

Sketch the Architecture of Accomplished Teaching from your NBPTS materials in the space below, and then answer questions 1-3.

1. When you look at the helix graphic in your NBPTS binder, you see that effective instruction begins with knowledge of your students. In what other ways do your Component 4 instructions correlate with the helix of accomplished teaching?

2. Where do you find that formative and summative assessment fit along the helix?

3. Match each of the steps in the helix to the <u>Overview</u> for Component 4.

What is the Helix?

The NBPTS has designed the Architecture of Accomplished Teaching©, which embodies the entire process of good teaching—not only in a sequence of instruction, as in Component 2—but also from year to year in the course of your career and professional growth. You will demonstrate how you bring your experience to your work to impact student learning, using an example of work with current students.

What is new to Component 4, as opposed to the old system, is the inclusion of your assessment practices. Another change has been the revised instructions that help you <u>focus</u> your work as a leader, learner, and collaborator <u>on student learning</u>, as <u>evidenced by data</u>.

What is Assessment?

<u>Let's Start with Self-Assessment</u>

We begin our discussion of assessment with the end in mind. Our assessment practices build until we help students become good at self-assessment. It is famously stated that "The goal of all assessment is self-assessment." In this component, you will be helping students with metacognition—which is thinking about how they think and learn. You will demonstrate your ability to help students plan, monitor, and assess their own understanding and performance.[1,2]

You will show evidence of how you help students take responsibility for their own learning. You will help them learn to OWN it and understand what to do with that.

What About Diagnostic Assessment?

We don't see much mention of diagnostic assessment in this component, but it's important to know the difference in diagnostic assessment and formative assessment.

They are similar in that they both provide a basis for planning and implementing instruction. However, diagnostic tests are often pre-tests that help a teacher understand where to start instruction, whereas other types of formative assessment often occur during the learning and help the teacher make adjustments during the lesson.[3]

Diagnostic assessment is one of the many forms of formative assessment; it tells you where to <u>begin</u> teaching, rather than how to continue teaching (unlike other uses of formative assessment.)

You might decide to mention or describe your use of diagnostic assessment as a part of your formative assessment practices in component 4, but make sure you focus your explanation of your work on other formative assessment, too. Include mention of the data you collect with any assessment.

What is Formative Assessment?

Formative assessment has become acknowledged as a very powerful method for producing significant learning gains.[4]

Formative instruction informs your next steps during the learning process. You will show how your ability to quickly assess your students' levels of understanding helps you differentiate for them and then adjust your instruction. You cannot formatively assess unless you are engaging with the students on some level.

Here's an example: If you use the "fist-to-five" strategy to determine whether to move on to a new concept, you might ask the students to hold up the number of fingers that represent how well they understand a concept (with five being an indication that they understand very well, or a fist indicating that they don't understand at all.) If all the students hold up four or five fingers, you might choose to move to the next topic. In this case, you have interacted with the students as you teach them.

Another example would be if you give the students "exit tickets" to complete before they leave the classroom. You ask them to write a definition in their own words for a concept you've studied that day. After they leave, you read what they have written to decide whether to continue the same concept tomorrow or whether you can build on today's learning. In this case, you are engaging with their writing, although they aren't present at the time. This formative assessment informs you about what you need to do next in your teaching of these students. A quote I like from a friend who trains teachers is that "If you don't do anything with the information before you move forward, it's not formative assessment."

There are many resources for examples of formative assessment on the internet, and a great thing about the National Board certification process is that it gives you an opportunity to try new ideas to see what works for you![5,6,7,8,9]

Tying It Up With Summative Assessment

Examples of summative assessments include chapter or unit tests, benchmark tests, semester tests, and state exams. These are used to measure the mastery of content or standards, and there is typically no time for students and teachers to adjust lessons or learning based on the data these assessment provide. Summative assessments measure outcomes rather than informing instruction. This is not to say that summative assessments aren't useful in prescribing next steps in a student's school career or future pathway.[10]

Challenge:

How could the figure below be used as formative and/ or summative assessment?

Photo by Jon Tyson on Unsplash

Questions for Reflection:

- In what ways have you used diagnostic, formative, and summative assessments in the past?

- In what ways have you helped students develop metacognition in the past?

- How can group work, work with peers, and projects help students develop the ability to self-assess?

- How might you be able to use self-assessment practices to help students understand how to plan for and improve their own learning?

- What questions do you still have about assessment?

References and Resources

1. Vanderbilt University Center for Teaching

   https://cft.vanderbilt.edu/guides-sub-pages/metacognition/

2. How Thinking About Thinking Can Help Kids

   https://childmind.org/article/how-metacognition-can-help-kids/

3. Diagnostic and Formative Assessments

   https://serc.carleton.edu/introgeo/assessment/formative.html

4. Diagnostic/Formative/Summative Assessment, Nuhid Y. Dumit, 2012

   http://website.aub.edu.lb/ctl/Documents/CLO%20summer%202012/Diagnostic%20formative%20summative%20asst.pdf

5. 56 Examples of Formative Assessment

   https://www.edutopia.org/groups/assessment/250941

6. 10 Innovative Formative Assessment Strategies

   https://globaldigitalcitizen.org/10-innovative-formative-assessment-examples

7. 12 Awesome Formative Assessment Examples

   https://www.aaeteachers.org/index.php/blog/1559-12-awesome-formative-assessment-examples

8. Fifty-four Different Examples of Formative Assessment

   http://cmrweb.gfps.k12.mt.us/uploads/2/7/3/6/27366965/formative_assessment_ppt.pdf

9. Examples of Formative Assessment

   https://wvde.state.wv.us/teach21/
   ExamplesofFormativeAssessment.html

10. Formative Vs. Summative Assessment

    https://www.aiuniv.edu/blog/2015/june/formative-vs-summative

11. The Literacy and Numeracy Secretariat Capacity Building Series

    https://www.uen.org/utahstandardsacademy/math/downloads/
    level-2/5-3-CapacityBuildingSeriesArticle.pdf

Photo by Dhruva Reddy on

Fast Track™ Chapter 4

Activity 4

Enter the criteria from the Level 4 Rubric from your Component 4 NBPTS materials in the data table below. An example has been done for you.

Evidence of:	1st evidence	2nd evidence	3rd evidence	other
Collaboration with families, caregivers and others to develop information				
Insightfully evaluates the information for relevance and relative importance				

Evidence of:	1st evidence	2nd evidence	3rd evidence	other

Evidence of:	1st evidence	2nd evidence	3rd evidence	other

Evidence of:	1st evidence	2nd evidence	3rd evidence	other

FastTrack™ Chapter 4

Activity 5

Activity 4.5— Essential Checklist for Component 4

Directions: For each question, circle Y for "yes" or N for "no."

1. I gained information about my student group through collaboration with parents, colleagues, community groups, or others in order to develop my student group profile. Y or N

2. I have evidence of <u>two-way communication</u> with parents. Y or N

3. I understand the culture of the students I teach. Y or N

4. I included data in my group profile that shows one or more <u>trends that establish a learning need</u> for the student group. Y or N

5. I can demonstrate that I designed instruction based on the data from diagnostic or summative assessments. Y or N

6. I can prove that I planned and implemented instruction based on data from assessments and then continued to assess formatively and adjusted instruction accordingly as a part of ongoing instruction. Y or N

7. I have evidence that I helped students make sense of assessment data and apply it to improving their learning through the feedback that I gave. Y or N

8. I can show evidence that <u>I helped students take ownership</u> of their learning. Y or N

9. I am able to submit evidence of professional development that I've taken part in as a LEADER, LEARNER, and/or COLLABORATOR in order to better serve my students (either my group and/or a larger group of students) to impact their learning. Y or N

10. I can demonstrate evidence that I have advocated for student needs that resulted in <u>measurable improvement</u> of student learning. Y or N

Video Access Information:

1) To access the videos, go to the following page,

https://vimeo.com/ondemand/fasttrack

2) Choose "Buy Videos" and enter promo code, CompleteSet

Do not pay additional money— the video access comes with the purchase of the book.

If you need assistance with any of these videos, please contact us at info@mynationalboard.com

Explanation of Terms

Accomplished teaching —NBPTS term for teaching that meets the Standards.

Architecture of Accomplished Teaching© —NBPTS graphic detailing the steps in accomplished teaching.

Assessment center— the standardized testing center where you will take your Component 1 test; you will register for a testing center near you after you have paid and the NBPTS sends you a "Permission to Test" letter. You must register by the January/February due date to test sometime between April and June.

Authentic engagement— the state of being intrinsically motivated to explore and learn the content.

Buzzwords— words that are current in educational discussions; words/topics that occur frequently

C1, C2, C3, C4 — abbreviations sometimes used by candidates for Components 1-4

Carol Ann Tomlinson— early researcher of Differentiation or Differentiated Instruction

Certification Area— this is very important; the National Board for Professional Teaching Standards areas for certification may or may not match the names of the certifications you have with your state. Be sure to check the nbpts.org website to find out "How to Choose Your Certification Area."

Clear, consistent, and convincing— the criteria for receiving a 4 out of 4 on an entry (component.)

Components— the four separate entries or tasks that comprise the National Board Process

Component 1 (C1)— Testing content knowledge and pedagogy for your certificate area.

Component 2 (C2)— Demonstrating your planning, implementation and results from teaching and analyzing student work from a sequence of instruction.

Component 3 (C3)— Demonstrating your ability to engage students in learning content while providing a safe, equitable, and challenging learning environment through video recorded evidence.

Component 4 (C4)— Providing evidence of your work as a leader/learner/ and or collaborator and your professional expertise as you gather knowledge of students that allows you to identify and address a student learning need. Demonstrating your intentional choices of professional development that help you grow/ or in which you help others to grow to meet and address or advocate for student learning needs. Especially important to demonstrate two-way communication and impact on student learning.

Constructed response questions (CR)— "essay questions" in which you have 30 minutes to answer a prompt at the assessment center. You will have three CR questions and 45 SR (selected response questions.)

Contextual Information Sheet— the form/ cover sheet for each entry that describes your teaching context so the assessor can visualize the conditions under which you are required to teach.

Diagnostic assessment— a form of formative assessment that helps a teacher understand where to begin instruction. Examples: pretests or kindergarten testing at the beginning of the year.

Differentiation— the act of varying teaching methods; also known as "D.I."

Differentiation of instruction vs. Differentiation for instruction— the former is changing methods of teaching for example, using technology rather than using group work or lecturing. The second is using various teaching methods that meet the unique needs of the individual students you teach; for example, if a student is interested in Power Ranger toys and you have had trouble helping him focus, you might choose to present letter sounds the child can associate with different Power Rangers when you are teaching one-one with him during reading.

Effective, Reflective Practitioner— this is the theme of C4.

Engagement (see also, student engagement)— student interaction with the content and with each other at the level of excitement and enthusiasm for learning. Engagement that results in a thorough exploration and attainment of the learning goals.

Entry (see components)— your component instructions from the nbpts.org website often refer to the components as "this entry…"

Evidence— each component requires you to provide clear, consistent, and convincing evidence that you have met the Standards on which you will be assessed.

Five Core Propositions© — These are the five basic principles outlining what Teachers Should Know and Be Able to Do. You can find this document in it's entirety on the nbpts.org website and it would be great to have read this the summer before you begin your candidacy.

Formative assessment— methods for gauging whether students are ready to move forward in a lesson or unit of instruction.

Helix— this is the short name for the Architecture of Accomplished Teaching©

Howard Gardner (see also, Multiple Intelligences)— the idea that there are many types of intelligence (8 Multiple Intelligences) was proposed by Howard Gardner and provides roots for the work of Carol Ann Tomlinson and other researchers in differentiation.

Impact on student learning— this is evidence that your planning and teaching have resulted in student learning. It can be qualitative or quantitative depending on the component and the questions to which you are being asked to respond.

Instructional context form— similar to the Contextual Information Sheet but this describes the exact lesson and students you are teaching rather than your school teaching context. They will probably not be the same.

Knowledge of Students— this is the basis for all your National Board work. The idea is that your planning and teaching must be based on these students at this moment in time. This includes an understanding of the personality of your class, understanding of each student in the class as an individual, and an understanding of the needs of this age of learner.

Leader/Learner/Collaborator— a "Big Idea" in National Board certification: the idea that teachers have a variety of roles in which they function professionally.

Level 4 Rubric— the highest score a candidate can receive is a "4" and the descriptors for the teaching that will result in this score is described in detail in the level for rubric. You can find this at the end of each component's instructions. Very specific to your certificate area and component.

Metacognition/ Metacognitive strategies— this is when a learner thinks about how he or she learns, including how to move forward in acquiring knowledge or meeting the learning goals. Teachers can develop an arsenal of strategies to help students acquire the skills of "thinking about thinking and learning."

National Board for Professional Teaching Standards (NBPTS)— a non-profit entity that developed the National Board Certification process and manages and monitors and publicly advocates for accomplished teaching. You can learn more at their website: nbpts.org

NB Standards (see also, Standards)— each certificate area has a lengthy document developed by teachers of that certificate area. This is worth reading because it outlines specifically the types of criteria your work will be measured against as your entries are scored. This document gives very specific examples of what accomplished teachers of each certificate area do. You will find that you already do many of the actions and activities and have much of the knowledge outlined. The thing to notice is how you normally demonstrate those competencies, and also when you know you do NOT do those things or have that knowledge. A key method of growth and achievement of National Board certification will be remedying your deficiencies through research and trying new things during your candidacy.

NBPTS binder— candidates typically prepare some kind of binder of their National Board components by printing them or downloading them and saving them to the desktop. This prevents problems if the website is difficult to access.

Pedagogy— the specific skills that teachers have in teaching content. Some of these skills are universal (such as questioning skills); others are specific to your discipline such as use of science inquiry lessons or writing strategies in ELA.

Professional Learning Need— this refers to C4; you will describe how you reached out for and integrated information that helped you in your teaching context or how you provided information for others so that you could impact students in some way. This is not random, but purposeful.

Reflection— Robert J. Marzano discusses the ability of teachers and other practitioners to act on the conditions in which they teach. Nurses are also reflective as they quickly assess and adjust for the unique situations in which they find themselves meeting the needs of their clientele. This reflective capability may show itself in the minute-to-minute adjustments a teacher makes, or in the more thoughtful analysis and deliberate adjustments a teacher may make at the end of a unit.

Safe, equitable, and challenging learning environment— referring to C3, you will demonstrate the decisions you make that help students feel safe; how you are equitable and encourage equity, and how you provide challenging learning opportunities for students.

Sequence of instruction— the timeframe varies by certificate area but is, for example, a segment of instruction that lasts 3-12 weeks. Sometimes called a "unit" of instruction. Important in C2.

Standards— see NBPTS Standards. These are different from your state mandated or Common Core Standards.

Student Engagement (see engagement)

Student Group Profile (also, Group Profile; Group Profile Form)— In C4, you develop a profile of a group of students using data and information and analyze it for trends that indicate a student learning need for the group.

Student Learning Need— as you analyze the trends in your Student Group Profile, you will be able to identify some common needs of that group that you can advocate for or address. This is important in C4 as you demonstrate both two-way communication and measurable impact on student learning.

Summative Assessment— typically this is the chapter assessment or unit assessment that comes at the end of the learning. It can even be a statewide standardized test, or an AP exam, etc. While it may be useful to determine a student's schedule for next year or next semester, the opportunity for the student to learn the material has usually passed. Assessments are specifically important in C2 and C4

Videos— in C3 you video record yourself teaching students.

Written Commentary— the instructions for each component have an Overview, a description of "What Do I Need to Do?" Other instructions, and a Written Commentary. These are the prompts found after all the other instructions that you will respond to using a set number of pages (usually around 12 or 13 pages) in which you describe, analyze, and reflect on your work for that entry.

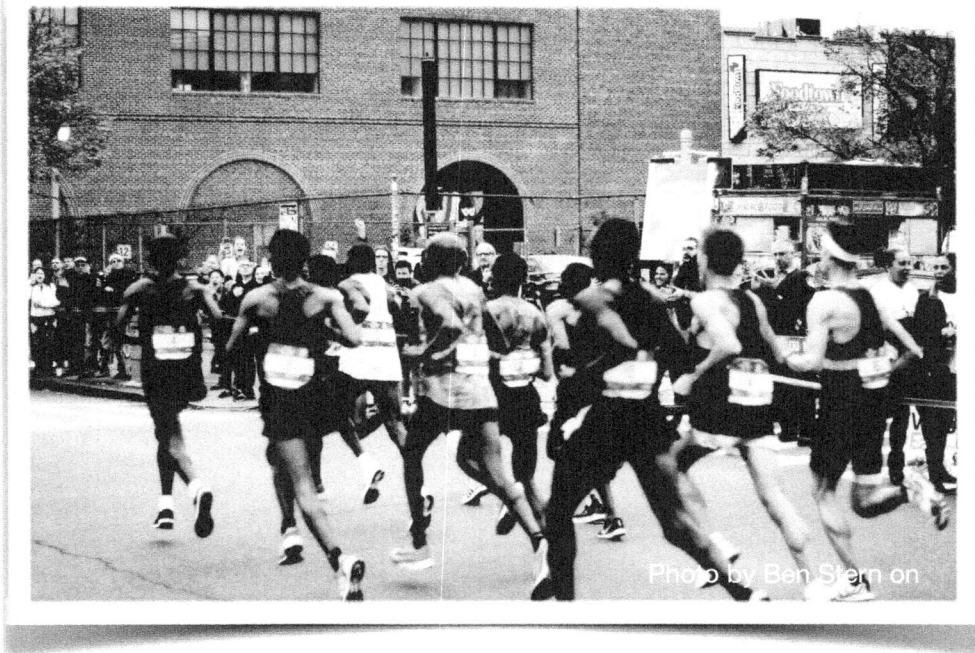

Photo by Ben Stern on

Made in the USA
Las Vegas, NV
17 June 2022